The Freelancer's Roadmap

Navigating the Gig Economy for Long-Term Success

Table of Contents

1. Introduction 1

2. The Freelancer's Landscape: Understanding the Gig Economy 2

3. Understanding the Gig Economy 3

   3.1. Growth of the Gig Economy 3

4. Characteristics of the Gig Economy 4

   4.1. Key Features of the Gig Economy 4

   4.2. Challenges in the Gig Economy 4

5. Strategies for Success in the Gig Economy 6

   5.1. Specialization 6

   5.2. Diversified Portfolio 6

   5.3. Continual Skill Building and Learning 6

   5.4. Self-Marketing 6

6. Mastering the Art of Finding Gigs: Top Strategies to Secure
Work 8

   6.1. Building a Marketable Skill-set 8

   6.2. Building Your Online Presence 8

   6.3. Using Freelance Job Sites 9

   6.4. Networking and Referrals 9

   6.5. Cold Pitching 10

   6.6. Constant Vigilance 10

7. Building the Perfect Portfolio: Showcasing Your Skills 11

   7.1. The Structure of Your Portfolio 11

   7.2. Choosing the Right Pieces 12

   7.3. Providing the Right Context 12

   7.4. Handling Confidential Work 12

   7.5. Managing Ongoing Updates 13

8. Networking in the Digital Age: Creating Fruitful Connections . . . 14

   8.1. Understanding Digital Networking 14

8.2. Getting Started: Building a Professional Online Presence 15

8.3. The Art of Digital Schmoozing 15

8.4. Expanding Your Network Through Digital Events 16

8.5. Building and Nurturing Relationships Over Time 16

8.6. The Challenges of Digital Networking and Overcoming

Them 17

9. Negotiation and Pricing: Getting Your Worth 18

9.1. Understanding Your Value 18

9.2. Streamlined Pricing Strategies 19

9.3. Foolproof Negotiation Tactics 19

10. Juggling Multiple Projects: Secrets of Successful Multitasking . . 21

10.1. Time Management: The Keystone of Success 21

10.2. Energy Management: Uniting Quality with Quantity 22

10.3. Organization: The Blueprint for Control 23

10.4. Communication: Your Freelancing Lighthouse 23

10.5. The Art of Saying 'No' 24

11. Dealing with Difficult Clients: Turning Challenges into

Opportunities 25

11.1. Understand the Potential Difficulties 25

11.2. Develop an Effective Communication Strategy 26

11.3. Set Boundaries and Manage Expectations 26

11.4. Harness the Power of Feedback 27

11.5. Cultivate Empathy 27

12. Financial Planning for Freelancers: The Path to Long-Term

Security 28

12.1. Setting Practical Financial Goals 28

12.2. Smart Budgeting for Freelancers 28

12.3. Understanding Taxes for Freelancers 29

12.4. Building an Emergency Fund 29

12.5. Retirement Planning for the Future 30

12.6. Investing for Wealth Growth 30

13. Keeping Up with the Market: Staying Relevant in a Rapidly Changing Economy 32

13.1. Unravelling the Flux of Market Trends 32

13.2. The Evolution of Skills and Technology 33

13.3. Utilizing Metrics, Analytics, and Reports 33

13.4. Diversifying Your Client Base and Revenue Streams 34

13.5. Honoring the Human Factor: Emotional Intelligence and Networking 34

14. The Freelancer's Future: Getting Ahead of the Curve in the Gig Economy 36

14.1. Reading the Market for Success 36

14.2. Upgrading Your Skills: The Lifelong Learner 36

14.3. Growing Your Network: Making Connections that Matter . . 37

14.4. Expanding Your Client Base: Multiple Revenue Streams 37

14.5. Staying Ahead with Top Tech Tools 37

14.6. The Power of Personal Branding 38

14.7. Planning for Financial Sustainability 38

Chapter 1. Introduction

Get ready to dive into, "The Freelancer's Roadmap: Navigating the Gig Economy for Long-Term Success," a special report brimming with insights that could revolutionize your journey in the exciting world of freelancing. This is more than just a report; it's your comprehensive guide to turning gigs into opportunities, juggling multiple projects with grace, and ensuring you're building a secure and prosperous future. Bumpy roads? Navigational nightmares? Not with us! Packed with expert analysis, actionable tips, and striking real-life case studies, this report isn't just theoretical — it's practical, engaging, and designed to equip you for triumph in the gig economy. Buckle up, because your roadmap to long-term freelancing success is just a click away!

Chapter 2. The Freelancer's Landscape: Understanding the Gig Economy

Let's start our journey by understanding the shape and nature of the freelancing landscape. The gig economy, also known as the freelance economy, was a steadily growing phenomenon even before the COVID-19 pandemic. Now, it's a tidal wave reshaping economies and changing perceptions of work throughout the world.

Chapter 3. Understanding the Gig Economy

Simply put, the gig economy is composed of short-term contracts or freelance work, as opposed to permanent jobs. In this new reality of work, freelancers provide services based on specific assignments, jobs, or 'gigs.' From app developers to virtual assistants, educators to artists, everyone's invited aboard this vibrant, bustling economy.

3.1. Growth of the Gig Economy

A combination of technology advances and changing attitudes towards work has fueled the growth of this dynamic economy. Mobile technology, high-speed internet, and robust online platforms have made it easier than ever to work remotely. It catalyzes the connecting of freelancers (sellers of services) with customers (the buyers). Alternatively, wider acceptance of flexible work styles, coupled with the desire for more work-life balance, has seen freelancers flourish.

To illustrate, studies suggest that the freelance workforce in the United States grew from 53 million in 2014 to 57 million in 2019. That's not a mere trend – it's an employment revolution!

Chapter 4. Characteristics of the Gig Economy

While the world of freelancing comes with attractive benefits such as flexibility, freedom, and independence, it also brings previously unfamiliar challenges like irregular income, job insecurity, and a lack of benefits. We'll be diving deeper into these facets as we progress.

4.1. Key Features of the Gig Economy

1. **Short-term engagements:** These can range from swift, one-time jobs to longer-term projects stretching over months. The defining feature here is their temporary nature.

2. **Flexibility:** Freelancers are often unhindered by traditional 9-to-5 schedules and can usually work at their own pace, in their chosen enviroment.

3. **Payment per project:** Unlike traditional employment, freelancers typically get paid after the completion of a project or the delivery of a service.

4. **Digital Platforms:** Online platforms like UpWork, Fiverr, and Freelancer.com are core pillars of the gig economy, connecting freelancers with potential gigs.

5. **Independence:** Freelancers are generally their own bosses, able to decide their work, their clients, and their rates.

4.2. Challenges in the Gig Economy

While the freedom and independence of freelancing can be alluring, it's crucial to also pay attention to its challenges, such as —

1. **Income instability:** Regular paychecks are replaced by variable incomes that depend on attracting and retaining clients. Job security is ditched for the hustle and grind chasing the next gig.

2. **Lack of benefits:** Freelancers, considered self-employed, often miss out on benefits like health insurance and retirement plans, normally provided by traditional employers.

3. **Increased competition:** The digital nature of most freelance work means competition isn't limited to your locality. You compete globally.

4. **Lack of job structure:** Being your own boss has its advantages, but it also means you shoulder all facets of running a business, from marketing to accounting.

Chapter 5. Strategies for Success in the Gig Economy

For some, these challenges are a small price to pay for the freedom and control that freelancing offers. But it doesn't mean you should stumble blindly into this new landscape. Adopting specific strategies can better equip you for long-term success.

5.1. Specialization

In a crowded market, specialization can help you stand out. Establishing a niche validates your expertise and can make you more attractive to clients looking for specific skills.

5.2. Diversified Portfolio

Reduce income instability by diversifying your client base. Rather than relying on one major client, successful freelancers foster relationships with multiple clients, providing a safety net should one client relationship end.

5.3. Continual Skill Building and Learning

The gig economy is ever-evolving, and standing still can lead to obsolescence. Regularly updated skills and knowledge keep you competitive.

5.4. Self-Marketing

Freelancers need to be their own cheerleaders. Promoting your work and abilities through a compelling portfolio and persuasive communication skills can attract more clients and better opportunities.

Remember, comprehending the landscape is only the first leg of the journey. As we progress further into the freelancing world, we'll explore more on how to tackle these challenges and gear up for the road ahead. From setting up your freelance business to dealing with financial management, you'll be fully equipped to navigate the thrilling course of the gig economy, straight towards success.

Chapter 6. Mastering the Art of Finding Gigs: Top Strategies to Secure Work

The key to thriving in the gig economy revolves around your ability to consistently secure work. Mastering the art of finding gigs requires more than just a stunning portfolio; it's about having a clear game plan that leverages your skills, networks, and digital platforms to your advantage.

6.1. Building a Marketable Skill-set

Transitioning into the arena of freelancing begins with knowing your worth. In other words, defining your marketable skill-set. What unique abilities and talents do you possess that set you apart from the crowd? Are you a developers who writes clean code, a dynamic social media marketer, a witty copywriter, or a top-notch graphic designer? Whatever your trade, you must know it, own it, and be prepared to sell it.

Assess yourself. You might possess a variety of skills, but identify which ones are most lucrative in the current market. Understand which skills are in demand, and harden those skills. Do not underestimate the importance of continuous professional learning. Up-skilling and cross-skilling are valuable strategies to stay competitive.

6.2. Building Your Online Presence

The next step is to build a prosperous online presence. Having a well-designed and regularly updated portfolio website is a good start. Showcase work samples that illustrate your talents, list services you offer, and include testimonials form satisfied clients if possible.

Professional networking sites such as LinkedIn are invaluable. Effectively leveraging them can open up a world of opportunities. Keep your profile updated, engage with relevant content, and make direct connections with professionals who might be interested in your skills.

Don't forget social media. Depending on your skill-set, platforms like Instagram or Behance could be more relevant. If possible, maintain activity on several platforms to increase visibility.

6.3. Using Freelance Job Sites

Freelance job boards are one of your most valuable resources. Websites like Upwork, Freelancer, Fiverr, and Guru provide platforms for freelancers to connect with clients from around the world.

These sites typically work by letting freelancers bid on jobs posted by clients. A word of caution: be selective about which projects you bid on. Ensure the task aligns with your skills and is worth your time. Stay away from clients with poor reputations or jobs offering unrealistically low payment.

6.4. Networking and Referrals

While much focus is given to digital avenues, don't overlook the power of networking and personal referrals. Connect with past clients, attend industry events, join local business groups, and get in touch with influencers within your niche. Word-of-mouth referrals carry a hefty weight since others back your credibility and vouch for your skill.

6.5. Cold Pitching

Cold pitching is an approach where you directly approach businesses or individuals, via email or other methods, proposing your services. It's uninvited, but it could be an effective technique if done right.

Ensure your pitch is personalized for the individual or company you're reaching out to. Show an understanding of their business and suggest specific ways you could help. Be concise, compelling, and always professional.

6.6. Constant Vigilance

You may have a steady stream of gigs, but don't rest on your laurels. The gig economy is unpredictable. It's crucial to always be on the lookout for your next opportunity. Fostering strong relationships with current clients can lead to more work. They may provide referrals or have upcoming projects of their own.

In conclusion, mastering the art of finding gigs is a multifaceted endeavor, requiring strategic thinking and proactive behavior. Inform yourself about the dynamics of the gig economy, and mould your strategies to suit them. Remember that success won't come overnight. But with patience and perseverance, you'll establish yourself as a successful freelancer with a steady stream of gigs.

Chapter 7. Building the Perfect Portfolio: Showcasing Your Skills

Creating an exceptional portfolio is the gateway to showcasing your skills and attracting a roster of high-quality clients. Regardless of what industry you are in, a well-structured portfolio serves as concrete evidence of your professionalism, experience, and talent. But constructing the perfect portfolio is more than just listing down your accomplishments or showcasing your work. It requires a strategic selection of material, thoughtful descriptions, and attention to aesthetics to effectively convey your unique selling proposition.

7.1. The Structure of Your Portfolio

Countless portfolio designs are abound in the digital world, but a successful portfolio essentially includes the following key elements:

- A Brief Introduction: This serves as your personal brand statement, outlining who you are, what you do, and your unique selling proposition. Keep it short, crisp, and impactful.

- Work Samples: This is the main reason people visit your portfolio—to see what you've accomplished. Choose projects that illustrate different facets of your skills and talent, and don't forget to include details of each project to give them context.

- Testimonials: Whether it's business, design, or writing, word-of-mouth remains a powerful tool. Include positive reviews from previous clients, making sure they are authentic and verifiable.

- Contact Information: Make it easy for potential clients to reach you. If applicable, also include your rates and working hours.

7.2. Choosing the Right Pieces

Not all projects are equal, and some will better highlight your skills and proficiency than others. Here's how to choose the best pieces for your portfolio:

- Relevance: Prioritize projects that align with your desired type of work. If you're aiming for website design gigs, for example, pick projects where you've excelled in this area.

- Variety: Show the breadth of your skills by including a range of different kinds of work.

- Quality over Quantity: It's better to have a handful of exceptional samples than dozens of mediocre ones. Choose your absolute best work for inclusion in your portfolio.

7.3. Providing the Right Context

Every piece you showcase should come with a context to help potential clients understand the scope and magnitude of your role in the project. Here's how to do it:

- Project Overview: What was the project about? Who was it for? When and where did it take place? What was its objective?

- Your Role: Clearly state your responsibilities and contributions to the project.

- Impact: Quantify your impact on the project. If you improved web traffic by 70% or saved a company $20,000, now is the time to state it.

7.4. Handling Confidential Work

Freelancers will likely handle projects with non-disclosure agreements or confidentiality clauses. Since featuring such projects could violate ethical and legal requirements, here's what you can do:

- Ask for Permission: Always consult with your client if you can include the project in your portfolio. Perhaps they'll allow you to showcase it with certain details redacted.

- Create a Replica: Replace confidential aspects of the project with fictional data. This way, you can still show off your work without breaking confidentiality.

7.5. Managing Ongoing Updates

Your portfolio is not a one-time task, but rather an evolving collection revealing your growth over time. To keep it polished:

- Routinely Audit: Regularly review and improve your portfolio. Remove outdated pieces and add new, brilliant projects.

- Highlight Recent Pieces: Prospective clients are most interested in what you've been doing recently, so ensure you're not only showcasing your best works, but also your most recent works.

- Prioritize Feedback: Encourage feedback from clients, peers, and mentors to continually refine your portfolio.

Creating a standout portfolio transcends just displaying your work—it's about narrating your professional story in a compelling way. Execute it well, and your portfolio will unlock doors to countlessly rewarding freelancing opportunities.

Chapter 8. Networking in the Digital Age: Creating Fruitful Connections

In the freelancing world, amassing a robust network isn't simply about knowing a lot of people. It's about creating meaningful, long-lasting connections that can lead to better opportunities and collaborations. As the digital age has advanced, so has the art of networking, transforming into something less intimidating and more accessible than traditional in-person meetings and conferences.

8.1. Understanding Digital Networking

Digital networking is the art of using digital platforms to form business connections, foster relationships, and maintain a solid professional network. Websites, blogs, forums, social media, and other online platforms collectively support successful digital networking, where you can reach out to a global audience as opposed to local events or meetups only that limit your networking efforts.

In the gig economy, digital networking isn't an option, it's a necessity. For freelancers, it equates to job opportunities, potential partnerships, and gaining access to resources and advice from seasoned professionals. Interestingly, your digital network can also serve as a support group; a digitized water cooler of sorts where you can share your struggles and victories with like-minded folks.

8.2. Getting Started: Building a Professional Online Presence

Before you start the networking process, you first need to establish a strong online presence. A professional, detailed LinkedIn profile is your digital business card and a great place to start. LinkedIn is a platform designed for sharing achievements and finding opportunities. Upload a headshot, write a compelling summary, and fill out your experience with as much detail as possible. Regularly sharing updates and engaging with other people's content will also help boost your visibility.

Not limited to LinkedIn, consider other social media platforms like Twitter, and Instagram, depending on where your target industry hangs out. Creating a professional website or setting up a blog showing off your skills can also help prospective clients or partners find you. The rule-of-thumb is to keep personal and professional social media separate, for the sake of protecting your brand and professional image.

8.3. The Art of Digital Schmoozing

True networking isn't about transactions but about building relationships, whether online or offline. Begin by creating a list of professionals who are in your field or associated fields. Follow them on social media, comment on their posts, share their work and if appropriate, initiate one-on-one conversations.

Another effective way to meet new professionals is by joining a digital community. There are numerous professional communities online such as Slack, Discord groups, or forums where professionals gather to discuss industry trends, share insights, and receive peer feedback. Find a few active communities, join in their discussions, share your ideas and if comfortable, share some of your struggles as well. There's no networking that matches bonding over shared experiences.

Never underestimate the value of offering help. If someone in your network queries about a challenge that you can solve, don't hesitate to pitch in your opinions or solutions. The logic is simple—give and you shall receive.

8.4. Expanding Your Network Through Digital Events

Webinars, online meetups, and virtual conferences are great places to meet and interact with professionals in your field. These are places where you can learn, share your insights, and connect with individuals or companies that might be on the lookout for freelancers.

Many of these events have chat rooms or comment sections where attendees can engage. Commenting thoughtfully and adding value to the discussions can make you more noticeable to others in attendance. Follow up with individuals after the event with a personalized connection request.

8.5. Building and Nurturing Relationships Over Time

Networking is a marathon, not a race. Building a strong, beneficial network takes time, persistence, and a willingness to offer value without expecting immediate returns. Always remember to follow up on conversations, deliver on promises, be helpful when you can, and remain patient.

A healthy relationship requires regular touchpoints. Regularly reach out to people in your network, share useful information, congratulate them on their victories, and engage with their online content. The goal is to ensure that when they need a service you offer, you are the first name that comes to mind.

8.6. The Challenges of Digital Networking and Overcoming Them

Digital networking isn't without its drawbacks. Reaching out to strangers can be intimidating, and it's not always easy to convert online relationships to real-world opportunities. But with perseverance, authenticity, and a helping mindset, the digital world can serve as a worthy platform for building and nurturing professional relationships.

While the landscape of networking in the digital age isn't always easy to traverse, it undeniably expands your reach and provides opportunities with greater flexibility. So remember, every comment, thread, or DM is potentially an open door. Gather courage, wear your professional best, and step into the bustling room—that is digital networking.

Chapter 9. Negotiation and Pricing: Getting Your Worth

Understanding and commanding your worth is pivotal for succeeding as a freelancer. Precise negotiation skills and efficient pricing strategies can make or break your career. Fortunately, arming yourself with some key insights and techniques can make all the difference. We'll break this invaluable information down into three comprehensive sectors: understanding your value, streamlined pricing strategies, and foolproof negotiation tactics.

9.1. Understanding Your Value

Becoming a freelancer implies breaking free of the traditional job market, where a specific position generally pays a defined salary. In the freelancing realm, determining your worth necessitates more than just comparing your qualifications against job descriptions. This exchange involves acknowledging, evaluating, and promoting your unique value proposition. It hinges on the exceptional skills, experiences, and perspectives you can bring to each project.

Firstly, audit your skills. This includes the professional abilities you've honed over your career, as well as the softer skills that make you a effective collaborator. Are you a master at creating engaging web content? Do you have a knack for interpreting complex data and making it accessible for every reader? Capture those talents as a part of your self-evaluation.

Secondly, consider your experience. This doesn't just encompass years spent in a given field, but also tangible achievements you've accomplished in that time. Did you brainstorm a campaign that increased website traffic by 50%? Were you responsible for a project which catapulted client satisfaction rates?

Lastly, factor in competition. What are other freelancers with roughly equivalent skills and experiences charging for similar services? Use this information as a benchmark rather than a definitive rule. Remember that undercutting competition isn't the only pathway to securing gigs. Clients often prioritize quality and reliability over minimal cost savings.

9.2. Streamlined Pricing Strategies

Making efficient pricing strategies is all about finding the balance between valuing your worth accurately, staying competitive in the market, and resonating with your client's budget. Here are a few strategies you may adopt:

Firstly, consider project-based pricing. Conduct a comprehensive estimate of the time and resources required to complete the respective project. Be sure to keep a buffer for unexpected twists and turns. This strategy provides clear expectations up front, and is ideal for clearly defined, finite projects.

Secondly, consider retainer contracts. These arrangements guarantee a regular, consistent income or workload. This can often bring more stability and security than a project-by-project basis.

Lastly, consider an hourly rate, especially if the project requirements are indefinite or are expected to change over time. This ensures you get paid for every hour you invest in a client's project.

9.3. Foolproof Negotiation Tactics

Now, you have a keen understanding of your value and you've identified a pricing strategy, but how do you secure that value through negotiation? Here are a few expert-recommended tactics:

Firstly, articulate your value explicitly. Succinctly convey what sets you apart and why the client will benefit from your offering compared to other options. Make this a centrepiece in your negotiation discourse.

Secondly, practice active listening. Understand your client's needs, concerns and 'pain-points'. Show empathy, but marry it with strategic problem-solving. Make it clear how your services can alleviate the issues the client is encountering.

Thirdly, never rush into giving a quotation. If need be, take your time in responding with a thoughtful estimate after assessing the project's scope, your value proposition, and market standards.

Lastly, do not be afraid to negotiate. Quiet your insecurities and remember that what you're offering has tangible value. Stand by your rates after having calculated them mindfully and logically.

Masterful negotiation and effective pricing are hallmarks of a successful freelancer. Adorn these tactics as your armour, and stride confidently into the battlefield of freelancing. Become a compassionate collaborator and a bold advocate for your immense worth. In the gig economy, you're a brand, and understanding, communicating, and standing by your value is paramount.

Chapter 10. Juggling Multiple Projects: Secrets of Successful Multitasking

In the vibrant realm of freelancing, a uniquely challenging yet rewarding aspect is the capacity to gracefully manage multiple projects at once. A pre-requisite for survival in the gig economy, it centers around effective multitasking, dotted with a few secret tips and tricks that can make the task significantly easier.

As a seasoned freelancer, the beauty of simultaneous projects is that it gives you a sense of security, diversity and an opportunity to stretch your creative boundaries. However, balancing multiple assignments might seem, at first, like juggling knives — risky, intimidating, and requiring exceptional skill. Yet like any art form, it's a matter of honing your skills and learning the ropes.

10.1. Time Management: The Keystone of Success

The keystone in the arch of freelancing success is time management. Acquiring proficiency over this seemingly intimidating term not only enhances productivity but also escalates overall efficiency. The essence of time management can be broken down into a few comprehensive steps:

- **Prioritize:** Devise a matrix to categorize tasks according to their urgency and importance. Crucial and immediate tasks come first, followed by important but not urgent ones, then urgent but not important tasks, and finally, the remainder. This Eisenhower Matrix simplifies decision-making and de-clutters your schedule.

- **Schedule:** Once your tasks are prioritized, feed them into your calendar. Follow the Golden Rule: Fill your most productive hours with your most crucial tasks. Adopting tools like Google Calendar or project management software can be immensely helpful.

- **Batch process:** Similar tasks are best tackled together. Designating specific time slots for similar assignments reduces cognitive load and enhances speed.

- **Stay realistic:** Remember, freelancers are humans, not machines. Overestimation can lead to unnecessary stress and under-performance. Strike a balance and be practical about your limits.

10.2. Energy Management: Uniting Quality with Quantity

While juggling several projects, meeting deadlines is as important as maintaining quality. This is where energy management intersects time management. It's about focusing not just on how long you spend on a task, but also when and where you allocate your energy:

- **Find your peak times:** Identify the periods when you're naturally the most productive — a boon when working on multiple tasks with distinct deadlines. Utilize these peak times for high-concentration assignments.

- **Use breaks wisely:** Remember the Pomodoro Technique – 25-minute work blocks with five-minute breaks. Rest revitalizes your mind, improving your productivity when you get back to tasks.

- **Exercise regularly:** Regular physical activity is known to increase your energy levels. A quick walk or yoga session between tasks can do wonders for your power of focus and execution.

10.3. Organization: The Blueprint for Control

An organized freelancer is a successful freelancer. More projects mean more details to remember – deadlines, client preferences, resource locations. Keeping track of these can be difficult without an organization system:

- **Project Management Tools:** Tools like Trello, Asana, or Monday can come in handy. They allow you to categorize tasks, assign deadlines, and monitor progress, all under one roof.

- **Digital Files Organization:** Establish a folder structure that makes sense – by client, by project, or by date. Naming conventions should reflect the contents for easy location in the future.

- **Keep communication centralized:** Keeping track of conversations, recommendations, and revisions can become a nightmare. Try keeping project-specific communication within project management apps, or organize emails into folders.

10.4. Communication: Your Freelancing Lighthouse

While steering through the stormy seas of freelancing, keeping open lines of communication is pivotal. It manages clients' expectations and keeps them in the loop about progress:

- **Regular Updates:** Send regular status updates, even if progress is as expected. This develops trust and exhibits professionalism.

- **Clarify Doubts Efficiently:** Seek early clarification if requirements remain unclear. It saves time later and prevents you from taking a wrong direction.

- **Handle Delays Professionally:** If you foresee a delay, communicate it proactively. Propose a new deadline and stick to it, to maintain your reputation.

10.5. The Art of Saying 'No'

The most difficult aspect for freelancers, especially beginners, is saying 'no.' However, it is essential to ensure quality work and prevent burnout:

- **Evaluate Before Accepting:** Assess each project vis-a-vis your skill set, interest, and the time it calls for before taking it up.

- **Respect Your Boundaries:** Understand your own work limits and ensure you're not compromising your health or personal life.

- **Negotiate:** If the scope of work is extensively huge or the timeline tight, negotiate. Either extend the deadline or divide the project into manageable parts.

No one masters the act of juggling overnight. Yet, with patience, practice, and persistence, you can become a freelancer who effortlessly multitasks, delivers quality work, and satisfies your clients. Remember, the road might be winding and steep, but the journey will be worthwhile. The gig economy awaits your talents. Show them what you're capable of!

Chapter 11. Dealing with Difficult Clients: Turning Challenges into Opportunities

Inevitably, freelancing comes with its fair share of tricky situations, which sometimes involves dealing with difficult clients. However, even these situations can morph into opportunities for personal and business growth with the right mindset and approach.

11.1. Understand the Potential Difficulties

Freelancers might coincide with a spectrum of challenging clients, each bringing their own set of complications. Some common types may include:

- The Over-demanding: These clients often have high expectations, with demands outstripping the remit of the job or your capacity.

- The Vague Visionary: They are not clear or decisive about their needs, leaving you with an ambiguous roadmap.

- The Micro-manager: They nit-pick every detail, often inhibiting the freelancer's creative process.

- The Ghost: A client who's inaccessible when you need their input or when payment is due.

Identifying which type(s) your client falls under will enable you to devise a suitable approach to manage the situation.

11.2. Develop an Effective Communication Strategy

Miscommunication, or lack thereof, is often at the root of difficult client relationships. Here's how to improve communication:

- Misunderstanding: Always ensure that both parties have the same understanding of the tasks. This can be achieved via regular check-ins or detailed briefs.

- Late Replies: Reinforce the importance of timely responses during the onboarding process. However, maintain respect for each other's personal time.

- Vagueness: Ask for detailed briefs. If they're unfamiliar with your line of work, provide a clear list of requirements or utilize a suitable questionnaire.

- Conflict: Stay calm, professional, and seek to understand their position before expressing your viewpoint.

11.3. Set Boundaries and Manage Expectations

Clear boundaries and expectations can significantly reduce challenges with clients:

- Define the Scope: Provide a detailed agreement that outlines the project's scope, deadlines, revisions, fees, payment terms, etc.

- Be Firm: Do not fear setting rules, limits, and standing your ground when clients overstep. It's crucial for your professional well-being.

- Over-Delivery: Over delivering occasionally is a great way to impress clients, but it can raise expectations for the future. Don't make it a frequent occurrence.

11.4. Harness the Power of Feedback

Negative feedback can sting, but it also provides vital cues towards improvement.

- Accept Criticism: Be open to it, understanding that it's the product that's under criticism, not you personally.

- Analyze Feedback: Analyze the feedback for clarity. If it lacks details, don't shy away from asking for specifics in a polite and professional manner.

- Take Action: When you receive justified criticism, implement changes. This shows sensitivity towards the client's needs and boosts your professional growth.

11.5. Cultivate Empathy

Empathy can break barriers, build trust and enable shared understanding.

- Put Yourself in Their Shoes: Understand the pressures and expectations your client may face.

- Keep Expectations Real: No client is perfect. Humans make mistakes, have bad days, and get moody. Treat your clients with a generous spirit of understanding.

In conclusion, difficult clients can be frustrating, demanding, and time-consuming. But, by understanding the client types, improving communication, setting boundaries, managing expectations, using feedback, and expressing empathy, you can create stronger relationships and successful outcomes. It's all about turning those challenges into opportunities and being better equipped for the diverse freelancing landscape.

Chapter 12. Financial Planning for Freelancers: The Path to Long-Term Security

The financial aspect of freelancing can be the most daunting for many. It's not just about earning money; it's about managing those earnings wisely to reap long-term stability and security. Let's first examine the importance of setting practical financial objectives, then proceed with an in-depth analysis on budgeting, taxes, creating an emergency fund, and investing for future security.

12.1. Setting Practical Financial Goals

It's crucial to begin your financial journey with a clear view of your goals. Financial objectives should be SMART – Specific, Measurable, Achievable, Relevant, and Time-bound. Understanding your financial targets can guide your strategies, spending, saving, and investing. For example, your goals may include saving for retirement, creating an emergency fund, buying a house, or affording a desired lifestyle.

Start by examining your financial landscape. Consider your current monthly expenditure, your earnings, and any existing savings and investments. From this point, you can start outlining your financial goals.

12.2. Smart Budgeting for Freelancers

Creating a smart budget is your next action point. As a freelancer, your income isn't always guaranteed, so it's important to budget for highs and lows. This irregularity in paycheck is why you need to formulate a budget that can withstand fluctuations.

While creating your budget, consider all your income sources, frequent expenses (like rent, bills, etc.), and irregular costs (like taxes, insurance premiums, etc.). It's advisable to overestimate your spending and underestimate your earnings to create a safety buffer.

Split your budget into three broad areas: regular living expenses, business expenses, and savings/investment. Tools like Mint, YNAB (You Need a Budget), and Quicken can help you keep track of your expenses and income.

12.3. Understanding Taxes for Freelancers

As a freelancer, you're responsible for calculating and paying your taxes. In most jurisdictions, freelancers need to send in quarterly estimated tax payments, made up of both income tax and self-employment tax.

In addition to the federal tax responsibilities, you may also have state tax obligations. The rates and rules vary, so it's recommended to check your specific state tax laws or consult a local tax advisor.

Consider using tax-preparation software like TurboTax or H&R Block, or hiring an accountant familiar with freelance tax requirements. Remember to pay your taxes promptly to avoid penalties and interest.

12.4. Building an Emergency Fund

An emergency fund is a financial safety net that can protect you during unforeseen circumstances such as illness, loss of a client, or a global pandemic impacting your freelancing gigs.

Financial experts often suggest saving for three to six months of living costs. Start creating this fund by setting aside a percentage of your income monthly. Once you reach your goal, it's helpful to continue adding to this fund.

12.5. Retirement Planning for the Future

Retirement may seem far away, but it's never too early to start planning. As a freelancer, the responsibility is on you to prepare for retirement since you don't have the benefit of an employer-sponsored retirement fund.

Types of freelance-friendly retirement options include Individual Retirement Accounts (IRA), Simplified Employee Pension (SEP-IRA), and Solo 401(k) plans. Choose what suits your earning pattern and future expectations best.

Robo-advisors like Betterment, Wealthfront, or human financial advisors can mentor you regarding retirement options relevant to your circumstance.

12.6. Investing for Wealth Growth

Investing is a practical way to grow wealth over time. However, investments come with varying degrees of risk, so it's essential to be informed.

Stocks, bonds, mutual funds, real estate, and peer-to-peer lending are some options to consider. You don't need to be a financial guru to start investing, but it's beneficial to learn the basics or consult with a financial advisor.

The act of financial planning as a freelancer could be overwhelming due to the sheer plethora of tasks. However, with the right approach to your finances – from practical goal setting, smart budgeting, understanding taxes, and financial safety nets, to retirement and investment considerations – you're paving your way to long-term security in the gig economy. Remember, it's a continuous process, not a one-time event. Devotion to financial planning can ensure your freelance dream does not turn into a financial nightmare.

Chapter 13. Keeping Up with the Market: Staying Relevant in a Rapidly Changing Economy

In the high-speed, ever-changing world of freelancing, staying relevant and competitive necessitates constant market awareness. Maintaining your relevance in the rapidly evolving gig economy isn't a choice; it's a necessity. It demands a proactive attitude, market savvy, and the willingness to adapt and learn continually.

13.1. Unravelling the Flux of Market Trends

Market trends are the thermometers of the economy. As freelancers, you are entrepreneurs in your own right, and decoding these patterns delivers a crucial advantage. As an initial step, note that trends exist at global, regional, and local levels.

Monitor news, listen to podcasts, follow influencers, and utilize online tools to keep your fingers on the pulse of your industry. Trends can range from massive waves, such as the seismic shift towards digital nomadism, to subtle trickles, like design style preferences in a specific niche.

Consider setting Google Alerts for relevant keywords, subscribing to industry newsletters, and regularly checking pertinent accounts on social media platforms. Participating in online communities, forums, and attending webinars or conferences – both virtual and physical – will ensure you're tuned into the buzz on the street level.

13.2. The Evolution of Skills and Technology

As technologies evolve, the demand for new skills increases. The fourth industrial revolution, ushering in advancements like AI, machine learning, data science, and more, has birthed a slew of emerging freelancing arenas.

In technology's immutable metamorphosis, harness the strategy of 'radical adaptation'. This involves not merely refining your current skills but also developing entirely new ones that match the zeitgeist.

There are abundant free and paid resources available for continuous learning. Platforms such as Coursera, LinkedIn Learning, Udemy, and Khan Academy amongst many others, offer courses on a wide array of subjects. Similarly, platforms like GitHub or Codecademy are excellent resources for those in the tech world.

However, it's not only hard skills that matter. Soft skills like communication, teamwork, critical thinking, and adaptability are all highly sought after in the modern freelancer. Balancing your skill set will make you a more attractive and versatile option for clients.

13.3. Utilizing Metrics, Analytics, and Reports

Metrics and analytics offer holistic overviews of your performance and can hint at market parallels. Regularly track and analyze your performance data to figure out your strengths, weaknesses, and opportunities. Predictive analytics can help forecast future trends and demands, helping you prepare and strategize accordingly.

Quantitative metrics are vital, but don't forget about qualitative ones – client feedback, for instance. Carefully analyze project feedback, client testimonials, or customer reviews. They offer a goldmine of insights into market expectations and can be essential pointers to where you need to level up.

13.4. Diversifying Your Client Base and Revenue Streams

"In this world, nothing can be said to be certain, except death and taxes" - Benjamin Franklin might as well have been speaking about the gig economy. Economic uncertainty is an inherent character of freelancing. To buffer against this unpredictability, diversifying your client base is crucial.

Having clients from a wide range of industries or sectors secures your income during industry-specific downturns. Similarly, offering a mix of long-term and short-term projects can guard against intermittent earnings.

In addition to diversifying your clientele, consider creating multiple streams of income. This can include a mix of active income (direct client work) and passive income (e.g., online course creation, e-books, blog monetization, affiliate marketing, etc.).

13.5. Honoring the Human Factor: Emotional Intelligence and Networking

In the digital age, we can forget about the human element of freelancing. Emotional Intelligence (EI) — the ability to understand and manage your own emotions, as well as empathize with others — is an essential asset in your freelancing toolkit. High EI can help maintain positive client relationships, manage stressful situations, and navigate negotiations effectively.

Another human-centric aspect that can't be underestimated is networking. Building relationships in the industry helps stay abreast of latest trends, provides learning opportunities from others' experiences, and even opens doors for potential collaborations. Attend networking events, engage on social media, and join industry-specific groups or forums. It's essential to remember that sometimes, it's not about what you know, but who you know.

In conclusion, staying relevant in the rapidly changing gig economy requires a multi-faceted approach. By tuning into market trends, continuously evolving skills, utilizing analytics and reports, diversifying your opportunities, and leveraging the human factor, you can remain a competitive and indispensable force in this dynamic landscape. Always remember - adaptability isn't about losing yourself; it's about keeping up with your environment to ensure your long-term success.

Chapter 14. The Freelancer's Future: Getting Ahead of the Curve in the Gig Economy

The gig economy has always been a transformative space. It's evolving sprawl promises growth and novelty but also throws up challenges for freelancers, requiring adaptability, resilience, and foresight. Harnessing the power of change thus becomes tantamount to getting ahead of the curve, setting the pace for future success.

14.1. Reading the Market for Success

As a freelancer, your survivability depends on your understanding of market demands. This comprehension necessitates an intensive reading and analysis of market trends, regular upgrading of skills, and effective networking within your field. Talk to industry insiders, follow thought leaders, be active in online forums, join relevant communities, create a rigorous reading list - all with the aim of gaining insights into market dynamics.

14.2. Upgrading Your Skills: The Lifelong Learner

Markets evolve rapidly, and freelancers who aren't on the growth path may find themselves obsolete. Continuous skill development is crucial. This doesn't mean just honing your existing capabilities, but also learning new skills that complement your portfolio and appeal to potential clients. Online education platforms offer opportunities for skills enhancement that can be leveraged for professional development. Remember, the more diverse your skillset, the wider the doors of opportunity will open for you.

14.3. Growing Your Network: Making Connections that Matter

Networking can be a gamechanger for freelancers. Building relationships allows for information exchange that can enhance your market understanding and open opportunities for collaboration or referrals. In the digital age, both local and global networking are possible and necessary. Online forums, social media, industry events and co-working spaces can serve as conducive platforms for building valuable connections.

14.4. Expanding Your Client Base: Multiple Revenue Streams

As a rule of thumb, freelancers should never rely on only one client or income source. The gig economy can be unpredictable, and having diversified income streams will ensure stability. Expanding your client base also fosters skill development, as each new project may require you to employ different tools or strategies. This diversity not only safeguards your financial stability but also sharpens your versatility.

14.5. Staying Ahead with Top Tech Tools

Technology is an asset freelancers can wield to their advantage. From project management apps to invoicing software, freelancers have an arsenal of digital tools at their disposal to streamline their workflow and increase productivity. Adapting to and adopting these resources can give you a discernible edge, enhancing efficiency and freeing up time for more strategic endeavors.

14.6. The Power of Personal Branding

In a crowded marketplace, personal branding helps freelancers stand out. It communicates your unique value proposition and drives recognition. Utilizing social media, a personal website, or blog can be invaluable tools in promoting your personal brand.

14.7. Planning for Financial Sustainability

A balanced approach to financial planning is critical for long-term success. Understanding your earnings, savings, investment strategies, and tax obligations is essential. Hiring a financial advisor can be worthwhile for complex finance management, while simpler budgeting can be handled with personal finance software or apps.

Getting ahead of the curve involves staying vigilant, always learning, connecting, standing out, and planning smart. The future can seem daunting, but equipped with these strategies and an open mind, freelancers can navigate the gig economy with ease and success.